AF351470

THE MYSTERY BEHIND THE Womb

EBENEZER OSEI BONSU

THE MYSTERY BEHIND THE WOMB
Copyright 2020© Ebenezer Osei Bonsu

No part of this book may be reproduced or transmitted in any form or by any means, electronic or mechanical, including photocoying, recording, or by means of any information storage and retrieval system, without permission in writing form the publisher/author. The use of short quotations or occasional page copying for personal or group study is permitted and encouraged. Unless otherwise stated, all scripture quotations are taken from the King James Version of the Bible.

Design and Formatting: Nonon Tech & Design

ISBN: 978-9988-3-0162-0

DEDICATION

To my mother, Akua Afriyie, by whose prayers and godly counsel, I have come thus far.

Table of Contents

Introduction

To begin with, it is important to mention that though the book principally addresses women, it is beneficial for everyone since we are all associated with women in one way or another.

The constant battle women go through has very little to do with men, which is contrary to the popular opinion that men are women's greatest "enemy". Men are not women's greatest "enemy"; most women suffer from identity crises. To a very large extent, it has caused most of them to bow down to the pressures of life more than anything else can do. The foremost solution to solving most of the challenges that stare us in the face is having understanding of the people we are made to be and what we carry inside of us. Identity crises begin most of the problems women go through in life. Emancipation is bred by awareness of one's identity and values. The worldview of most women will alter the day they discover their real identity. The attempt of this book is not to discredit men or to belittle their value as authoritative figures as God accorded them. The intent is to rather set the records straight that women are unique and different in their own special way, and to get the best out of them, they must be respected and treated with care.

Biologically, many things set women apart, but I think the most unique thing is *"the womb"*. The womb is a mystery on its own and that's the greatest target of the devil since the beginning of the world. The word "woman" connotes womb-man. This implies that it is the womb that distinguishes women from men. There may be several other differences, but the womb distinctively sets women apart.

Women are the devil's greatest enemy of all the things God created. The war against women began in Genesis 3:15; God said, *"And I will put enmity between you and the woman, and between your seed and her Seed; He shall bruise your head, and you shall bruise His heel."*

Every woman, consciously or unconsciously, is in a never-ending battle with the devil. This message from God was actually the most heart-breaking news the devil received after he rebelled against God. God said, *"...the Seed of the woman shall bruise your head..."* This can be paraphrased as follows: *"Devil, what can hurt you badly will be carried by the woman in her womb."* This news began the war against women. The devil is not against women because of how beautiful they were made; neither is it because of their hips nor butts. His main headache against women is the *"womb"* they carry. It is for this reason that he has risen against several destinies, especially that of women. He knows if he allows any woman to go through life without launching an attack against her, his kingdom will be under siege.

The only *"power"* to conquer Satan and his cohorts is given to any Seed that forms inside of the womb of women. It is for this reason that the devil deploys so many attacks, particularly, against women in all areas of their lives just to get their wombs corrupted. His reason for doing that is that a corrupted womb will definitely produce a corrupted Seed. Matthew 12:33 reads: *"Either make the tree good and its fruit good, or else make the tree bad and its fruit bad; for a tree is known by its fruit."* A bad tree will most definitely produce bad fruits. It is easy and common for a prostitute to give birth to a prostitute. Ezekiel 16:44: *"Indeed everyone who quotes proverbs will use this proverb against you: 'Like mother, like daughter!' ..."* It is highly possible for someone to give birth to her kind.

The descendants of Eve became sinners, not for their own sins but because they came from a corrupted and a sinful womb. David understood this when he said, *"Behold, I was brought forth in iniquity, and in sin my mother conceived me."* (Psalm 51:5)

It has been the desire of Satan to get every womb corrupted. If women will understand this war against them and their place in carrying God's Heavenly agenda on earth, through the womb they carry, they will from today preserve themselves. The destiny of every nation rests on the shoulders of women. Women give birth to nations. God told Rebekah, *"Two nations are in your womb; two peoples shall be separated from your body..."* (Genesis 25:23). It is clear from what God said that women are carriers of nations. No nation succeeds when it fails to treat her women as Queens.

Chapter One

THE WOMB
– THE GATEWAY TO THE WORLD

"And behold, thou shalt conceive in thy womb, and bring forth a son, and shalt call His name Jesus."
(LUKE 1:31)

The only place that validates a person before he gains access to the world is the womb. God specially designed the womb as the only gateway to the world. The ticket to be called a Human Being is given through the womb. It is abnormal for one to be born from outside of the womb. Women are the only gateway to the world. This is the reason why God could not defy such a divine law in His attempt to save mankind.

Jesus could have come through any other means without the womb, but that could have rendered Him unqualified for the fulfilment of God's purpose. God clearly ignored the role of a man in the process, but He didn't ignore the role of a woman. Mary, the mother of Jesus, confirmed that she was without a man, yet God used only her to bring His Son into the world *"…How shall this be, seeing I know not a man?"* (Luke 1:34)

The Angel of God said, *"Behold, you shall conceive in your womb and bring forth a Son, and shall call His name Jesus."* Take note that the conception took place in her 'womb' and not any other part of her body. It was the womb that gave Jesus credibility to live on earth as a human being and enabled him to identify himself with human beings. One difference I know between the devil and Jesus Christ is that Jesus had a legal birth which permitted Him to live on earth, but the devil entered the earth illegally. This is why we have the power to cast the devil out of any place he finds himself; be it our business, family, health, etc. Unlike Jesus, the devil has no right to live in any part of the world or in anything because he didn't come through the womb.

Among all the things God created, women are exceptionally unique. Without them, no one qualifies to live. The day men will acknowledge the dignity and value of women will be the day they will be liberated in all their endeavours.

God created all things under the sun, including animals of different kinds, trees, fishes, etc.; and gave man dominion over them. Man had everything to make life beautiful and pleasant, yet he was not content and satisfied. His state was still considered incomplete. God then intervened to make a helper suitable for him – *"And the Lord God said, it is not good that the man should be alone; I will make him an help meet for him."* (Genesis 2:18) For God to begin, He removed a rib from the side of the man, formed the woman and brought her to him. Here is the mystery: Eve came in to make Adam's world good and complete. God said, *"It is not good that man should be alone…"* It means that the woman God brought to Adam had all that man needed to feel good and live fulfilled. The condition of man before the woman came in was declared bad, as God testified. The first statement Adam made upon seeing the woman was: *"This is now bone of my bones and flesh of my flesh…"*

None of the things God created had the similitude and nature of Adam. They all belonged to different classes such as birds, cattle, fishes, etc. God brought the woman to fill the vacuum that was left in the man's world. The man is in no way greater than the woman in anything. The fact that they are *'the weaker vessel'*, as the Bible describes them, doesn't make them less in importance or weak in anything. The Bible meant they are precious and therefore need to be treated with care and respect. The permit to live in the flesh is given to them. It will be a great disservice to men to mistreat and look down on women.

MISCONCEPTIONS ABOUT WOMEN

Several misconceptions have been raised about women since the fall of mankind. I have heard terrible things being said about women. Many people have held on to the traditions of men and, thus, speak anyhow against things God fashioned out of excellence. God never created the woman to be a slave to the man; neither was the man created to be a slave to the woman. We are all made equally in God's image. The woman has a command to submit and the man, on the other hand, is commanded to love (Ephesians 5:22–29). There is no law that supports men to see women as less in creation. They both had an equal mandate from God, and that is, to have *"dominion"* over all other creation: *"Then God blessed them, and God said to them, "Be fruitful and multiply; fill the earth and subdue it; have dominion over the fish of the sea, over the birds of the air, and over every living thing that moves on the earth."* (Genesis 1:28). In accordance with the Bible, it is clear that the dominion was handed to both Adam and Eve. Since it wasn't given to only the man, men should never try to exercise their mandate of dominion over women, who are fashioned out of excellence as suitable helpmates. Being a helper is not equal to being a servant. That perception is the devil's attempt to paint women black to men. Unfortunately, he has succeeded in polluting the minds of people to incubate that thought, which is totally against the will of God for mankind. Now, let's look at some of the commonest misconceptions about women.

"Women allowed the devil into the world."

The devil's entry into the world has nothing to do with human beings. God, the Master of creation, masterminded it. Lucifer, who became the devil, became so full of himself when he realized that he was endowed with so much power and magnificence. He planned a coup d'état in heaven with the aim to overthrow God. He said, *"I will ascend above the heights of the clouds, I will be like the Most High"* (Isaiah 14:14). This thought of pride and arrogance incurred the wrath of God, which made the Arch Angel Michael stand against him, and his Angels and prevailed against them. The Bible states the following: *"So the great dragon was cast out, that serpent of old, called the Devil and Satan, who deceives the whole world; he was cast to the earth, and his angels were cast out with him"* (Revelation 12:9). The devil was cast out from Heaven because of the thought he incubated to overthrow God. It wasn't women who allowed the devil into the world. Before God made Adam and Eve, the devil was already a fallen Angel. Eve did nothing to influence his coming. It was his pride and arrogance that barred him from Heaven.

"Women are devils."

Human beings are made expressly in the Image of God. God took His time to form and mould us out of the dust and He breathed into our nostrils the breath of life to enable us represent Him on earth. Among all the things God created, only humans had the privilege to share in His image. The very nature of God is in us; that is why He spent quality time to work on us. He could have called us into being just as He did with the other creation. It is important, therefore, to note that neither Adam nor Eve had the seed of the devil or resembled the devil in any form. Eve was the last creature God made, and His work was perfect. No wonder the man exclaimed in delight: *"This is now bone of my bones and flesh of my flesh; She shall be called Woman, because she was taken out of Man"* (Genesis 2:23). The excitement in the man's voice can clearly be noticed. It is noteworthy that if the woman was taken out of man and we believe the lie that she is a devil, it presupposes that the rib God took from the man was already infested by the devil. Women are not devils and they can never be. Men only need wisdom to handle them well. The woman is herself a mystery to the man because before God formed her, He had to put the man into a deep sleep. Man saw nothing in the formation of the woman and, therefore, cannot make any allegation regarding what she's made up of. It is an error to call something or someone you are ignorant about evil. Men will only need knowledge and understanding before they can live with women (1Peter 3:7).

"Women are cheap."

This is perhaps the commonest of the misconceptions raised about women. It is far below the belt for someone to describe women as cheap. No creature of God is cheap, except, of course, we fail to understand the purpose for which that creature was made. When God finished His creation, He saw everything He created to be very good and priceless: *"Then God saw everything that He had made, and indeed it was very good..."* (Genesis 1:31). It is true that the devil has succeeded in stealing the hearts of some women as he has done to some men; however, we still cannot, and should not, see them as cheap in any way. To be cheap is to be inexpensive because of low quality or value. This definition doesn't befit women. We cannot generalise all women under one bigger umbrella. The fact that some women have lost their dignity and pride doesn't mean they have all lost them.

Unfortunately, some women have failed to live up to expectation, but that still doesn't give credence to tag all women as failures. Many are making every second count in their world for good. The godly women are still virtuous and priceless, and they will do nothing to soil their reputation. They are those the Bible calls *'priceless'* in Proverbs 31:10: *"Who can find a virtuous wife? For her worth is far above rubies."* It will be a mistake for someone to try to put them in a negative class. The Bible again says in Proverbs 18:22 that *"He who finds a wife finds a good thing, and obtains favor from the Lord."* There is something about women most men have not yet discovered. The few who have discovered it are benefiting. The saying that *"Behind every successful man there stands a woman"* isn't a fallacy or a myth. It contains a great deal of real truth. This is in line with our previous scripture that *"He who finds a wife finds a good thing."* Undoubtedly, there is something good and wonderful about women. The keys to unmake and make men are in the hands of women. However, it will depend on how the latter are treated.

<u>"Women are not wise."</u>

Women have been the backbone of men since the creation of the world. It takes men of understanding and knowledge to fully grasp that. Every society that has overlooked the value of women never progresses; so is every man who insults and mistreats women. My Godfather once told me in a very funny way, *"Only a fool can say women are useless."* There are communities across the globe, especially in some parts of Africa, where women are relegated to the background; they are not allowed to talk when men are talking. Besides, in decision-making, women hardly have the chance to make suggestions or inputs. Their designated place is the kitchen and the bedroom. However, it is ironic to see those same men, who don't respect their women, leaving their children in the care of those same women when going to work. How can someone perceived to be unwise raise wise kids?

Clearly, the number of hours women spend with children is more than that of men. Consequently, women's influence on children far outweighs that of men. That's why most children naturally grow with very deep affection for their mothers. It is because of the number of hours mothers spend with them and the motherly care they receive from mothers. Calling our women '*foolish*' simply means that the training they give our children is full of folly. This would therefore imply that everyone raised by a woman is foolish; however, in reality, we know that is not the case. A man is not greater than a woman in anything. The truth is that God has assigned everyone a unique role, which distinguishes people from others. Women can do whatever women are expected to do, and the same applies to men. Due to the uniqueness of the two sexes, there is no need to compare them.

A typical example is a man in the Bible who considered himself wise and, thus, despised everyone, including his own wife. He never included the wife in any decision he took. That act almost cost him his life. It took the wise intervention of the same woman he never respected to save him from death.

"The name of the man was Nabal, and the name of his wife Abigail. And she was a woman of good understanding and beautiful appearance; but the man was harsh and evil in his doings. He was of the house of Caleb." (1 Samuel 25:3)

In terms of character, the man we are describing here was a direct contrast of his wife. Whereas the wife was meek and good, the man was proud and evil. However, with wisdom, Abigail could live with such a man.

"Now one of the young men told Abigail, Nabal's wife, saying, *"Look, David sent messengers from the wilderness to greet our master; and he reviled them...Now therefore, know and consider what you will do, for harm is determined against our master and against all his household. For he is such a scoundrel that one cannot speak to him."* (1Samuel 25:14–17)

In the above passage, Abigail was informed of her husband's misbehaviour towards David. Being a woman of understanding, she quickly saddled her ass to go out and clean her husband's mess. These were her words when she met David, *"Please, let not my lord regard this scoundrel Nabal. For as his name is, so is he: Nabal is his name, and folly is with him! But I, your maidservant, did not see the young men of my lord whom you sent."* (1 Samuel 25:25) Her wise counsel stopped David from shedding blood: *"And David said to Abigail, blessed be the Lord God of Israel, which sent thee this day to meet me: And blessed be thy advice, and blessed be thou, which has kept me this day from shedding blood, and from avenging myself with mine own hand."* (1 Samuel 25:32–33)

Abigail operated in the wisdom of God. There are countless women time would not permit me to talk about, who have risen above the ranks to become giants in their fields of endeavours. Like Nabal, lots of men have met their untimely death because they disrespected the women God blessed them with. There are countless women who operate in a higher capacity of wisdom even more than Abigail.

WHY WAS IT EVE INSTEAD OF ADAM?

As the Akan proverb has it, *"A tree that bears good fruits shall always be pelted."* Those who came up with this proverb realised, after many years of experience, that it is not strange for things and people with good prospects to face challenges. This implies that a person's level of greatness determines the accompanying level of attack. The truth is that there is always a hidden agenda for any attack the devil projects. He has never attacked anyone without having a goal.

This brings us to the question: Why did Satan confront Eve though Adam was in the Garden? He had a perfect reason for doing that. He could have gone to Adam, but he rather went to Eve, knowing what he was going to get, should he succeed in deceiving her. We are going to be looking at why he chose to go to Eve.

INFLUENCE

The Bible clearly refers to the devil *"old serpent"* since his existence is not new. He will not start an attack if it will not bring any profit to his kingdom. He is very tactical in everything he does. No wonder one-third of the Heavenly Beings were manipulated by his deceits.

The power to rule was handed to Adam since he was created before Eve (1 Timothy 2:13). However, the influence of that power was handed to Eve. God intentionally designed women in a way that their mere appearance can influence men. Women carry an electrifying presence; that's why even a mad woman can get impregnated by a sane man. The Master Craftsman perfectly moulded women to be classic with all their body parts uniquely arranged. The attractiveness that comes with their shape alone can lure a man into doing things that he wouldn't usually do.

The truth is that no matter how powerful a man is, his power can melt into the hands of a woman. God naturally made it so. For instance, Samson was the strongest man who ever walked the earth. With regard to physical strength, there has never been a man of his calibre. He could carry a whole city gate and climb a mountain with it. Besides, he subdued a whole army with the jawbone of an ass. Nothing could tame him, and no Giant could withstand his might. Not even the whole army of the Philistines could stand him. The nation of Israel actually enjoyed the greatest freedom during the rule of Samson because no enemy dared invade their territory. Nevertheless, the million-dollar question is as follows: What became of his might and his divine assignment to live as a warrior? Sadly, the answer is *"No!"* The purpose for which he was born was terminated prematurely by the influence of one woman called Delilah. He was ultimately reduced from being a Mighty Warrior to a dancer in the presence of the people he once conquered. What a shame! What ridicule!

The Philistines drew a strategic plan that could quickly bring Samson to his knees, after all their efforts to conquer him had failed. The execution of the plan was to be spearheaded by a woman; therefore, they contracted a woman called Delilah, whom Samson had fallen for. As recorded in the Bible, *"…the lords of the Philistines came up to her and said to her, "Entice him, and find out where his great strength lies, and by what means we may overpower him, that we may bind him to afflict him; and every one of us will give you eleven hundred pieces of silver."* (Judges 16:5)

The contract the lords of the philistines gave Delilah was simply to entice him and find out the source of his uncommon strength. The question is: What made them come up with the idea that a woman could do that job for them? The answer is simple: it was because they knew from experience that the power of a woman's influence far outweighs the physical strength of a man. If the solution could come from physical strength, they had the calibre of Goliath in their camp; however, that was not the case. It was about a special electrifying presence which God placed in only women. The work which took men of strength so long to do was easily done by Delilah. She succeeded in influencing

Samson to reveal the source of his strength, a secret God had warned him never to disclose to anyone. Samson effortlessly disobeyed God due to a woman's influence. This is the same strategy most of the multimillion companies have been using over the years. By the charming presence of women, they get people to buy their products without a second thought. Women have more power over men than any other creature of God.

Another intriguing instance was about the children of Israel. They grew stronger and powerful as a nation. No attempt to destroy them worked; not even a spiritual attack could bring them down. The reason was because they had God on their side. Strangely, in their journey to the Promised Land, they were confronted with a powerful nation called Moab. The Moabites' fear of being wiped off made them go and hire the service of a Prophet with the assignment to curse them on their behalf. The Prophet did all he could to bring them down spiritually, but he failed. He ended up blessing them instead. These were the Prophet's words after all attempts had failed: *"For there is no sorcery against Jacob, nor any divination against Israel. It now must be said of Jacob and of Israel, 'Oh, what God has done!'* (Numbers 23:23)

However, the prophet offered a timely counsel that consequently brought the children of Israel down. He counselled the Moabites to send their women into the midst of the Israelites to influence them to play harlotry with them and to give up on their God. This counsel became so influential that the Israelites turned their backs on their God.

"Look, these women caused the children of Israel, through the counsel of Balaam, to trespass against the Lord in the incident of Peor, and there was a plague among the congregation of the Lord." (Numbers 31:16)

Just the influence of women caused the children of Israel to do the unthinkable and impossible. They were compelled to follow other gods and they made great sacrifices to lifeless altars. Their nation almost collapsed and came to naught. There are several instances where women influenced powerful nations and people to do what they had not thought of doing. It was the power of this influence vested in women that made Eve the target when the devil entered the Garden of Eden; he then succeeded in using her to get the man without toil.

Chapter Two

THE WOMB
– SATAN'S TARGET

t is noteworthy that the womb of women, which is their greatest asset for the world, is, at the same time, their biggest problem. Satan's hatred against women is simply because of the womb they carry. He attacks the source of every blessing, and that was what he did to Eve. Satan realised that it was through the womb of the woman that the blessings God pronounced on the human race was going to be fulfilled: *"Then God blessed them, and God said to them, "Be fruitful and multiply; fill the earth and subdue it; have dominion over the fish of the sea, over the birds of the air, and over every living thing that moves on the earth."* (Genesis 1: 28)

The devil hates the idea of humans multiplying and subduing the earth. It was his greatest fear because every seed that comes out of the womb of the woman is a potential threat to his kingdom. This implies that humans multiplying and subduing the earth translated into the fall of his kingdom, hence the attack on Eve.

THE RAGE AGAINST WOMEN

Revelation 12:17: *"And the dragon was enraged with the woman, and he went to make war with the rest of her offspring, who keep the commandments of God and have the testimony of Jesus Christ."*

Satan hates women with passion. That is why every woman should develop herself spiritually. Every woman, no matter how she is, so long as she carries a womb, is at war with Satan and his allies. The war against women started after God had made the following declaration in Genesis 3:15: *"And I will put enmity between thee and the woman, and between thy seed and her seed; it shall bruise thy head, and thou shalt bruise his heel."*

It makes women naturally enemies to Satan. In this case, it doesn't matter whether one has erred or not; women are at war with Satan. The womb women possess is the enemy's greatest problem with them. This is why he has succeeded in deceiving some women to go through surgery to have their wombs removed and totally change their appearance to be called 'transgender' men. According to the decree God made, women naturally have what it takes *"to bruise the head of the serpent [Satan]"*. Women are naturally powerful, thanks to their wombs.

Revelation 12:1–17 brings out a startling mystery about an incident which took place in Heaven. It describes a pregnant woman who was due for delivery; her appearance alone was a wonder as we read. She was clothed with the sun, she had the moon under her feet, and upon her head was a crown of twelve stars. Simply, the woman was decorated with honour, power and influence. This should be the description of every woman. Women are uncommon and powerful. It is an error for any woman anywhere to look down on herself. The appearance of women alone is something to behold. God took His time to perfect them since they were the last to be made, and were so precious to Him as well.

As the woman was ready to deliver her baby, the Bible records, another wonder appeared in Heaven, which was a great red dragon representing Satan. Get it! There are only two wonders in all of God's creation: Women and Satan, as the scripture points out. Satan appeared because the woman carried something that had the DNA, according to the pronouncement of God, to overcome him. In order words, he came there with gross anger because the woman carried in her womb the seed which is infused naturally with power to crumble his kingdom. Satan was ready to devour the woman and her baby. Revelation 12:4 *"And his tail drew the third part of the stars of heaven, and did cast them to the earth: and the dragon stood before the woman which was ready to be delivered, for to devour her child as soon as it was born."*

Every woman must understand that the womb is the greatest threat to Satan and his demons and they will do everything in their power to destroy the carriers of it. The devil knows that if he succeeds in destroying just one woman, he has succeeded in wiping a whole generation. Generations are inside of every woman. This is the reason why women must take their spiritual lives to the next level to stop the devil and his attack. Every seed that drops in the womb of every woman has the power to overcome the devil. This is why the devil fights women from a very young age to ensure that they lose their virginity and also become promiscuous and godless. In that case, he gets an upper hand on every seed that drops in the womb. He simply can't afford the destruction that will hit his kingdom if women are delivered from ignorance and rather take their place as Influencers. It's therefore not surprising to see girls as young as 18years and below engaged in all sorts of abominable things such as abortion, lesbianism, prostitution, etc.

The rage the devil has against women is unimaginable. He will not spare any woman who does not pray, but is godless and careless. Women are precious and carry something that poses the greatest threat to the devil; he has an idea of what women carry and what they are made up of. Women remain a mystery and a wonder to men.

A godly woman has more influence on her generation more than a godly man does. The godliness of women coupled with their influence can affect millions of people, unlike men. For instance, when a man wants to sell something to a woman, the woman can easily choose to reject it without a second thought, which is not the case when a woman wants to sell that same thing. A woman can easily sell an idea, a product etc. to a man without him thinking of the consequences. Her appearance will first do the selling, then her soothing voice before she even begins to present the product. Women possess a natural charm from God.

The truth is that the devil is after every woman, whether small or big. The reason is that winning one woman in his kingdom can bring about 1000 men. Again, corrupting one woman would mean that every seed that falls inside her womb will most definitely be corrupted.

MAKERS AND DESTROYERS OF KINGS

Women have what it takes to make and unmake men; it will depend on how people treat them. Women can be very helpful, caring, loving, gentle, resourceful and supportive. That is when they meet men who handle them as Queens. For instance, no matter how beautiful a car may look, if you put water where you're supposed to put petrol, there is no way it will respond. Men will need knowledge to stay with women: 1 Peter 3:7 states that *"Likewise, ye husbands, dwell with them according to knowledge, giving honour unto the wife..."*

Knowledge is a condition of being aware or studying to know. Women don't need just any man; they need men of knowledge to handle them. Whoever is ready to relate and mingle with women must go for knowledge. Living successfully with women ultimately calls for knowledge. This is why many men have had issues with women; they thought women need only money and other material things to survive. A man of knowledge will know what every woman needs, and one of the greatest is honour. Women can do everything to have honour and can behave anyhow if they're refused it. In honour, we find respect, care and attention. These are the things we must give women to get the best out of them. Every woman has the keys of kingship in her; it will take a man of knowledge to successfully have that key.

Women who destroy Kings

No woman is born evil. Situations and circumstances mould them to be so. For example, tigers are wild and dangerous when you meet them in the jungle; however, they can be very gentle when kept as pets in people's homes. The difference is that the tigers in people's homes are given some treatment that those in the forest normally lack. For instance, unlike the tigers kept as pets, those in the forest fend for themselves, no attention is given them and they have no honour from the outside. This makes them see anything around them as a threat and an enemy. Depending on how women are treated, they can be savage tigresses in the jungle or tame tigresses in people's homes.

Some men have pushed their women to the level of becoming destroyers. For a woman to get to that point, it implies there will be hell around whoever might have caused it. This is why there's no peace in some homes and offices since the women who are supposed to be treated as Queens are being trampled upon. If you live around a woman who has been made a destroyer, there will be no peace for you. Men's drunkenness, poverty, instability, etc. can sometimes be attributed to the women in their lives who are making things tough for them. Women have in them what can change every man's life positively or negatively. Sadly, they have the potential to ruin a whole generation, if they are pushed to do so. It's like a coin of two sides, and the side that shows is determined by how the coin is treated.

In my own estimation, women hold about 85 percent of every man's life. Why God took just a rib from man's side to form woman is a mystery, but since then, every man who comes into the world must also come from the inside of women. Women give birth to men and feed them till they grow into independent adults. Usually, when it's time for marriage, they entrust themselves again into the care of women until death. Thus, it is very dangerous for a woman to be pushed into becoming a destroyer instead of being a helper. Since the devil is aware of this, he fights so hard to sow that seed of destruction in women to make life miserable for men.

It is easy for women to ruin kings when they are refused the honour they deserve. Every man who thinks no woman has the power to destroy him must be joking. You don't treat someone who controls the higher percentage of your life as a nonentity and expect to succeed in life.

Women who are Kingmakers

I have heard several men attributing their success to the women in their lives. It is true that the state of every man who has respect for women and treats them as Queens is something glorious to behold. God pronounced that it is not good for man to live alone. God then created the woman and brought her to the man to enhance his life. This means that any man with a woman in his life is more likely to make it in life, depending on the way he treats that woman. Men succeed when they get the maximum peace of mind and comfort to pursue their dreams. Such peace lives in the heart of women. The moment a man finds a virtuous woman, progress is released into that man's life and everything he does succeeds. Women are naturally made mothers to men. The comfort, care, love, attention, prayers and advice they give can make an ordinary man extraordinary.

Proverbs 18:22: *"Whoso findeth a wife findeth a good thing, and obtaineth favour of the LORD."*

The word of God is forever settled! We can neither make additions nor omissions. The word of God is clear on the value of women. As the Bible points out, any man who finds a wife finds a good thing. This means that the word 'wife' or 'woman' is synonymous to the word 'good'. If the journey of success is three steps, finding a woman means you have obtained the first step. The other thing God adds to you after finding a woman is favour. Favour is the flavour that God adds to one's life to bring speed. When you have favour, obstructions are erased; thus, it can take just a day for you to obtain what people spend years to obtain. For God to say that about women, it means there is something about them that men have not yet discovered.

For a man's prayer to even be accepted by God, it depends on the way he treats women. 1 Peter 3:7: *"Likewise, ye husbands, dwell with them according to knowledge, giving honour unto the wife, as unto the weaker vessel, and as being heirs together of the grace of life; THAT YOUR PRAYERS BE NOT HINDERED."*

It is easy for a man who is made a king at home by his woman to become a king outside his home. It is said about the virtuous woman that *"Her husband is known in the gates, when he sitteth among the elders of the land."* (Proverbs 31:23)

The 'gate' in that context is the world of business. His woman supports him, not only to be recognised, but also to get the best deal in his transaction. No wonder *"Her children arise up, and call her blessed; her husband also, and he praiseth her."* Proverbs 31:28

Many men have risen through the ranks to be a force to be reckoned with, because of some women they encountered in their lives. Women are kingmakers and can easily make a useless man a King within the shortest possible time.

Chapter Three

THE WOMB
– THE FACTORY OF MIGHTY MEN AND WOMEN

There are known manufacturing factories across the world that produce many products of high quality. The truth is that those factories don't come near the womb in terms of production. The womb remains the greatest when it comes to the production of quality Men and Women. There is no normal human being born in the history of the world that is not a product of the womb. The womb houses great men and women for about 9months until they are born to the world. Every known great person spent about 9months in the womb. This is why the devil has never been happy with any seed that drops inside the womb.

He works tirelessly to destroy women in order to get rid of their wombs in order to prevent them from bearing babies.

Revelation 12:13: *"and when the dragon saw that he was cast unto the earth, he persecuted the woman which brought forth the man child."*

Mighty men and women have emerged in the religious sphere, the corporate world, the world of entertainment, science, academics, etc. These people include inventors, preachers, revivalists, educationists, etc. Time will fail me if I attempt to mention names of people who have done excellently well in shaking demonic kingdoms and contributed greatly to benefit their fellow humans. None of these came into the world from outside the womb. They are all products of the womb.

The Angels of God kept Mary safe throughout her pregnancy, because the devil was after her life. Mary kept herself pure for the Lord and for His assignment in her entire life. There was not even a single chance the devil got to use her in any way to defile her womb. The devil knew the seed she carried was going to be a threat to his kingdom. He pursued Mary so hard, but God was on her side. When the time for her to be delivered was due,

God fashioned everything in such a way that the only place available to them caused Jesus to be born in a manger. Understandably, if the delivery had taken place elsewhere, the devil could have worked through attendants to have Mary or the Baby killed.

Luke 2:6–7: *"And so it was, that, while they were there, the days were accomplished that she should be delivered. And she brought forth her firstborn son, and wrapped him in swaddling clothes, and laid him in a manger; because there was no room for them in the inn."*

Any woman who's living her whole life to please God is a threat to Satan and his kingdom. God is always on her side to protect and deliver her. The devil could harm neither Mary nor her Child, though he did everything he could. He even tried using kings to have the Baby and His mother killed, but they failed.

Matthew 2:13–14: *"And when they were departed, behold, the angel of the Lord appeareth to Joseph in a dream, saying, Arise, and take the young child and his mother, and flee into Egypt, and be thou there until I bring thee word: for Herod will seek the young child to destroy him. When he arose, he took the young child and his mother by night, and departed into Egypt."*

In terms of bearing quality men and women, the womb remains the greatest asset to mankind. That is why the devil fights women tooth and nail by driving them into prostitution, promiscuity, abortions, barrenness and premature death.

WEAPONS WOMEN NEED TO CONQUER MEN: LOVE AND WISDOM

Don't be scared by the heading! I want to set some records straight to women everywhere. This is to show women a more appropriate way to take back their place as Queens. Many women of our time have resorted to several strategies and techniques in their bid to have freedom and change the status quo, but unfortunately, those strategies seem not to be working for them. There are several associations of women, whose ultimate goal is to fight for freedom and demand for respect in this society of ours which is full of male chauvinists. Countless conferences have been held by women's groups to demand for equal platforms with men, but it seems the desired results have not been achieved yet. Marriages are in disarray as women can't figure out what they can do to tame their husbands. Most women even go to the extent of fighting, insulting and denying their husbands sex just to feel superior and be recognised. The truth of the matter is that women are missing one important weapon that can easily get them the results they are requesting for. The WEAPON OF LOVE and WISDOM is the most efficient and powerful weapons women can use to defeat men in any confrontation.

No amount of insults can change a man, EXCEPT LOVE and WISDOM. Our women seem not to be winning their battle against men because they fight instead of being LOVING and WISE. What they should take note of is that fighting men only makes them stronger and less sensitive. Men have naturally been created with physical strength, which makes it difficult for any woman anywhere to win with physical tantrums. Obviously, some women would say they have tried severally and demonstrated enough love but it has changed nothing. The truth is that the weapon of LOVE has the power to weaken any man, if it's used by women WISELY. Women must learn a great deal from Queen Esther in the book of Esther.

In the Book of Esther, we read an interesting story about Haman whom the Bible describes as the Jews' greatest enemy (Esther 3, 10). This man did all he could to get the approval of the then King, who was Esther's legal husband, to kill all the Jews in his kingdom, of which Esther was part. The king granted his request, but had no idea that it was about Queen Esther and her people. When Queen Esther became aware of Haman's evil plot, she could have acted swiftly in her capacity as a Queen to have him destroyed. However, she applied WISDOM and rather decided to show LOVE.

She went to the king and, upon seeing her, the king asked her to request for anything she wanted, even up to half of his kingdom. Though Esther could have quickly asked the king to annihilate Haman and all his descendants *(Physical means)* She rather asked the king to come with Haman to the Banquet she had prepared for the two of them *(Weapon of Love)*

Esther demonstrated love towards the man she had every reason to disrespect and destroy. That simple act of Esther got her all her needs. Esther set a table before the man she knew was a torn in her flesh. She was so nice to Haman that he felt so loved and even went home to tell his wife about his awesome experience at the palace (Esther 5:12). No wonder God fought for her. Women, let Love and Wisdom lead because they are the most effective WEAPONS that can be used to overpower Men.

It is rather unfortunate that some women who are aware of these weapons use them negatively. A typical example is of Delilah. Though she behaved badly, there is something positive every woman must learn from her story. Delilah never gave up using love tactics until she won. She couldn't have won if she had used insults, quarrels and fighting. It would have been impossible for her, since Samson was physically way stronger. Delilah knew it and deployed the WEAPONS OF LOVE and TACT, which made Samson bow to her and reveal his greatest secret. Women don't have to fight for significance; they are naturally made significant. This is a secret which the devil is even aware of and, therefore, shudders.

If women will know and understand this and start using the weapons of Love and Wisdom, men from all walks of life will easily give in to them. The moment women begin to use physical means through fighting and insults, they are headed for failure. The power of every woman to conquer is in the magnitude of the love she can demonstrate at every point in time. There is no weapon stronger and mightier than the weapon of Love. It's in the nature of every woman to love, and that's the greatest weapon God purposefully put inside them.

From my childhood till now, I have never seen a woman who won her battle over her man with insults, curses, quarrels, etc., especially in marriage. The lives of Esther and Delilah teach us that the only way to tame a man who is strong in drunkenness, sexual immorality and other forms of vices is to employ love, tact and wisdom.

Chapter Four

WEAPONS WOMEN NEED TO CONQUER SATAN

Every woman is a target of the demonic kingdom. The strategies they put in place aim at getting women trapped so they will influence several men and get them into their cage. Women are more powerful than they can imagine. In Eden, the devil ignored Adam and rather went to Eve. He knew what he wanted from Eve; and truly, when he had her, it became easy to get Adam. This is how powerful women are. Satan doesn't play with his attack on women and we should remember that all his attempts to trap them aim at having control over the womb, so that he can control any seed that is conceived.

Revelation 12:15: *"and the serpent cast out of his mouth water as a flood after the woman, that he might cause her to be carried away of the flood."*

He wants every woman to be carried away in his flood of deception. Though many women have already become victims, this is a wake-up call to bring them back on their feet. God is always on the side of those who are willing to make every day count. There are six weapons women need to employ to render Satan powerless.

The weapon of a Dedicated Life

This is a weapon the devil can't withstand at all. A woman who has her life dedicated to God can never be oppressed by the devil. They mark those women as their no-go areas. Dedicated women live purposefully and know what they ought to do to remain on fire and committed to God.

Their devotion is their greatest priority and they will sacrifice everything for it. Such women will not fall for anything that doesn't meet the standards set by the Word of God. A Dedicated Life is a weapon that leaves no space for the devil to occupy and misbehave. It is a life that's fully surrendered to God. James 4:7: *"Submit yourselves therefore to God. Resist the devil, and he will flee from you."*

Such women have God as their All in All and don't mind being ridiculed due to their reliance on Him. Their commitment and devotion form a top notch. The devil flees when he sees them.

Women who refuse to live for God fall for anything, including the charms and deceits of the evil one. Every woman should emulate Mary, the mother of Jesus. She left no space for the devil to operate. She had her whole life dedicated on the altar of God. These were her words after she received tidings from Heaven: *"And Mary said, Yes, I see it all now: I'm the Lord's maid, ready to serve. Let it be with me just as you say. Then the angel left her."* (Luke 1:38 TMB)

For women to boldly declare *"I'm the Lord's maid, ready to serve..."* means they know what they are about and the glory they are made to exude. The devil is afraid of such women and he will dare not play around them.

The weapon of Prayer

Prayer is an act that invites the Host of Heaven into the affairs of the earth. Women who make prayer their lifestyle hardly have the devil playing with their lives. Prayer causes Heaven to intervene in the helplessness of men. No demon tries his hand on anyone who has the backing of Heaven. Prayer does not only make us fearless and bold; it also strengthens our relationship with God.

Hannah's prayer broke the yoke of barrenness placed on her by Satan and she had Prophet Samuel as a result. (1 Samuel 1:10)

Prayer can do what no human strength can achieve. There is an extraordinary force behind the prayer of the Saints that no demon can ever withstand. When women go down on their knees to pray, the kingdom of Satan is set ablaze. For any man to succeed, despite hindrances, it means a woman somewhere is standing in the gap to intercede for him; On the other hand, when men are failing, it means their women are failing their assignment as intercessors. The greatest gift every man can have is a prayerful wife. Having Women in prayer is the greatest force people can benefit from. They pray from the deepest part of their heart, which quickly draws the attention of Heaven.

Praying women are empowered women. They are able to handle their spiritual affairs without anyone's intervention. It is said of Susana Wesley that she spent two hours each day to commune with God in prayer. Her prayers and dedicated life paved a way for her children. Generations are kinder with their verdict for her impactful life. Charles Wesley wrote over 6,600 hymns, and John Wesley is hailed as one of the most powerful, renowned and greatest Evangelists who walked on earth. They were formed by their mothers' unceasing prayers. The devil is not concerned when women are doing well physically, that is, in terms of beauty, academics, etc.; however, he's seriously concerned when women can pray. Esther brought the greatest enemy of the Jews, Haman, down through her prayers (Esther 4:16). The energy emitted from the prayers of women is fervent and more powerful than any artificial force. Hebrews 11:35: *"Women received their dead raised to life again..."* These were not ordinary women. Their lives were defined by prayers, so the devil feared to lay his cold hands on their children and other relations. The devil is put to flight anytime women stand to pray.

The weapon of Holiness

Holy living is not a life devoid of problems, but a life that's lived in Christ Jesus. Such people emulate Christ Jesus. Holiness is a life without blemish, spots or wrinkles. Ephesians 5:27: *"That he might present it to himself a glorious church, not having spot, or wrinkle, or any such thing; but that it should be holy and without blemish."*

The devil is always on the lookout for things he can use to accuse women. Staying spotless and being without blemish is one of the surest ways to cause him to stay out of one's life. John Wesley once said, *"Give me one hundred preachers who fear nothing but sin, and desire nothing but God, and I care not a straw whether they be clergymen or laymen; such alone will shake the gates of hell and set up the kingdom of heaven on Earth."*

A life that is spotted cannot defeat the devil. Women who fear nothing but sin can successfully overthrow the kingdom of Satan and completely ramshackle his agenda. 1 Peter 3:5: *"For after this manner in the old time the holy women also, who trusted in God, adorned themselves, being in subjection unto their own husbands."* Holiness is a potent weapon every woman can use to stop the evil hands of the devil.

The weapon of Virginity

Virginity is not only the state of a woman who has never had an affair with a man. It's a shield also against Satan. Virgins have their lives naturally immune against demonic destruction, especially when they are born again. The devil is seriously afraid of women who remain chaste until they are married. Godly and chaste women have their wombs highly secured and their glory intact. God couldn't have used any woman but a godly Virgin to fulfil His promise to humanity. Luke 1:26–27: *"And in the sixth month the angel Gabriel was sent from God unto a city of Galilee, named Nazareth, to a virgin espoused to a man whose name was Joseph, of the house of David; and the virgin's name was Mary."*

Mary was not only a virgin, but had her life dedicated to God. This doubled her protection, so no attempt of the devil against her life came to pass. Among the Jewish people, virgins were cherished and highly honoured. 2 Samuel 13:18: *"And she had a garment of diverse colours upon her: for with such robes were the king's daughters that were virgins apparelled..."*

The garment of diverse colours was designed to set virgins apart. They were not to be compared with other women who had illegally broken their seal of virginity. It was not for nothing that they designed such apparels for virgins. That was physical apparel which announced their uniqueness to the world. In the same vein, spiritually, there is a covering on virgins; they are protected and sealed. Have you asked why occultists ask for the blood of virgins for rituals and other demonic sacrifices? They are exceptionally unique in the spirit world; therefore no altar, including demonic altars, rejects them.

The weapon of Worship

I grew up to see my mother as a worshipper. She uses worship to fight all her battles. She will wake up early dawn each day and begin to reverently worship God. You can literally feel the presence of

God when she begins to worship. This act makes her a successful woman in all her endeavours. Worship is to honour with extravagant love and extreme submission (Webster's Dictionary, 1828). It does not only take place in songs; our lifestyle also worships God. Worship breaks into pieces demonic afflictions. Isaiah 54:1(TMB): *"Sing, barren woman, who has never had a baby. Fill the air with song, you who've never experienced childbirth! You're ending up with far more children than all those childbearing women." GOD says so!"*

How can singing make a barren woman become fertile? It tells us that some songs can break yokes. These are not ordinary songs, but songs that reverently magnify God. The promise God has for every worshipper is in Isaiah 54:13: *"And all thy children shall be taught of the LORD; and great shall be the peace of thy children."* Worship has a compelling force that draws God to take over from our hands. Instead of using your human skills to train your children and others, God promises to do that for you at no cost, through your simple act of reverence.

Paul and Silas in prison deployed the weapon of worship and the answer was amazing.

Acts 16:25–26: *"And at midnight Paul and Silas prayed, and sang praises unto God: and the prisoners heard them. And suddenly there was a great earthquake, so that the foundations of the prison were shaken: and immediately all the doors were opened, and every one's bands were loosed."*

The devil is afraid of worshippers. When women go before God with their hearts soaked deeply in Worship and Praises, their answers come in torrents. 2 Chronicles 20:22: *"And when they began to sing and to praise, the LORD set ambushments against the children of Ammon, Moab, and mount Seir, which were come against Judah; and they were smitten."* Worship defeats Satan.

The weapon of Sacrifice

Sacrifice is a powerful weapon to stop the hands of Satan and release Heaven's fragrance. Women like Mary, Martha, Salome, Dorcas and many others lived their lives making sacrifices to Jesus and His disciples. They did so well that Jesus couldn't forget them. Women who understand sacrifice carry some unusual presence.

2 Kings 4:8–10: *"And it fell on a day, that Elisha*

passed to Shunem, where was a great woman; and she constrained him to eat bread. And so it was, that as oft as he passed by, he turned in thither to eat bread. And she said unto her husband, Behold now, I perceive that this is a holy man of God, which passeth by us continually. Let us make a little chamber, I pray thee, on the wall; and let us set for him there a bed, and a table, and a stool, and a candlestick: and it shall be, when he cometh to us that he shall turn in thither."

The woman whose name is not known was said to be a Great Woman, not because of her wealth and influence but because she understood sacrifice. She was willing to share her wealth with the people of God. She fed Elisha and his servant and even provided shelter for them. This act ended her years of barrenness, when the man of God spoke over her life. There is nothing we give to God that goes unrewarded. Every act of sacrifice receives the attention of Heaven. Hebrews 6:10: *"For God is not unrighteous to forget your work and labour of love, which ye have shewed toward his name, in that ye have ministered to the saints, and do minister."*

Ministering to the needs of the saints and orphans

is one of the surest ways to open the Heavens over one's life. Mark 12:44: *"For all they did cast in of their abundance; but she of her want did cast in all that she had, even all her living."*

The widow sacrificed her last money to God because she understood the importance of sacrifice. I don't think her life remained the same after that act. Women who have lived their whole lives making sacrifices to God and to the people of God have had their children's lives secured by God. The woman who gave Elijah a whole room and fed him for months had her child attacked by the devil, but God remembered her sacrifice and the child was brought back to life. (2 Kings 4:32–36)

Conclusion

The battle line has been drawn. So long as the earth abides and women continue to have wombs, the war between them and Satan will never cease. This is not about what you did or did not do; so long as you're born a woman, you're in an unseen battle with unseen enemies. Women are the devil's greatest threat. He gets paranoid any time he sees women making every second count for God. This is what he has been about ever since he and his accomplices were barred from Heaven.

Revelation 12:17(NLT): *And the dragon was angry at the woman and declared war against the rest of her children—all who keep God's commandments and maintain their testimony for Jesus.*

Everything Satan does is geared towards getting women into his trap. Every woman needs to wake up to this mystery and act before it becomes late.

The only safe place to keep women from the evil one is in God. There is no way the devil can defeat any woman who is grounded in the Lord. The devil is extremely afraid of such women and will not dare touch anything which has their seal of prayer.

To a large extent, this book has endeavoured to open our eyes to the mysteries surrounding women. It is up to us to act and make a conscious effort never to allow ourselves to be wounded by his projections. Satan is cunning and will not spare any woman who lives carelessly. His attempt is to trap women and use them as baits to get several men. In so doing, he corrupts the womb and gets an upper hand over every seed that falls into it. Women who keep themselves from being defeated by the evil one eventually succeed in preserving their children and subsequent generations.

Psalms 112:2–4(NLT): *"Their children will be successful everywhere; an entire generation of godly people will be blessed. They themselves will be wealthy, and their good deeds will last forever. Light shines in the darkness for the godly. They are generous, compassionate, and righteous."*

As a woman, anything you do either opens a door for the devil to attack you or closes a door against him. The truth has been presented; get hold of it and apply it so that you can live above Satan and his attacks. Women are significantly priceless and their value in the world can't ever be downplayed. They control the world with their God-given influence. Let's all help them keep this treasure so that present and future generations can benefit from all the good potentials God has deposited in Women.

About the Author

EBENEZER OSEI BONSU is a prolific writer, a passionate worship leader and a counselor. He obtained a bachelor's degree in Development Education Studies at the University for Development Studies and holds Masters in Theology at the Evergreen Bible College. He serves the body of Christ with his special prophetic and healing grace.

He is the founder of the Students Christian Fellowship on the University campus, a vibrant fellowship that has grown to train several leaders for Ministry. While studying at the University, he was awarded the most influential Student for his extraordinary service towards people of all class.

As a servant leader, he understands where people are and reaches out to them. He is a voice in this generation that encourages, informs and comforts men and women with godly counsel.

www.ingramcontent.com/pod-product-compliance
Lightning Source LLC
Chambersburg PA
CBHW061339120726
48001CB00002B/934